Breaking the Darkness

A Journey of Healing and Recovery from Depression

Dr. Jilesh

About the Author

Dr. Jilesh is a renowned and highly rated manifestation expert, spell caster, psychotherapist, life coach, and master of business administration. With extensive experience and expertise in the field, Dr. Jilesh has garnered a reputation as a trusted authority in the realm of manifestation and personal transformation.

As a highly rated manifestation expert and spell caster on Fiverr, Check Global Reviews here - https://www.fiverr.com/jileshthilakan?up_rollout=true[1] Dr.Jilesh has assisted countless individuals in manifesting their desires and achieving their goals. Through his deep understanding of the principles of manifestation, Dr. Jilesh has helped clients tap into their innate power to create their dream reality.

In addition to his work on Fiverr, **Dr. Jilesh has also excelled as a highly rated instructor on Udemy, with more than 30k students** Check his personal development courses here - https://www.udemy.com/user/jilesh-thilakan/ [2]sharing his knowledge and empowering students worldwide to harness the power of manifestation. With a passion for teaching and a commitment to providing valuable insights, Dr. Jilesh has garnered a loyal following of students who have experienced transformation and success under his guidance.

Dr. Jilesh's expertise extends beyond manifestation, as he is also a qualified psychotherapist and life coach. His background in psychology and counselling allows him to provide holistic support to individuals seeking personal growth and transformation. Through his empathetic approach and profound insights, Dr. Jilesh helps clients overcome challenges, break through limiting beliefs, and create lasting positive change in their lives.

Furthermore, Dr. Jilesh holds a master's degree in business administration, which adds a unique perspective to his work. His understanding of business principles and strategies allows him to guide individuals in aligning their personal goals with professional success, creating a harmonious balance between their aspirations and career pursuits.

With a diverse skill set and a genuine passion for helping others, Dr. Jilesh is committed to empowering individuals to unlock their full potential and manifest a life of abundance, fulfilment, and joy. Through his teachings, guidance, and transformative techniques, he aims to inspire and support others on their journey towards manifesting their deepest desires and living their best lives. **For more about Author checkout his Blog-** https://www.healingoraclewisdom.com/

---

1. https://www.fiverr.com/jileshthilakan?up_rollout=true
2. https://www.udemy.com/user/jilesh-thilakan/

Copyright © 2023 by Jilesh Thilakan

All rights reserved. No part of this book may be reproduced, distributed, or transmitted in any form or by any means, including photocopying, recording, or other electronic or mechanical methods, without the prior written permission of the copyright holder, except in the case of brief quotations embodied in critical reviews and certain other non-commercial uses permitted by copyright law.

For permissions requests, write to the publisher at the address below:
Publisher: Dr.Jilesh, India
Website: www.psychologyquill.com
Email: drjilesht@gmail.com
Cover design by Jilesh Thilakan
Cover image: Jilesh Thilakan

Disclaimer: The information contained in this book is for educational and informational purposes only. It is not intended as a substitute for professional medical advice, diagnosis, or treatment. Always seek the advice of your physician or other qualified health providers with any questions you may have regarding a medical condition. The author and publisher disclaim any responsibility for any adverse effects resulting directly or indirectly from the use or application of the information contained in this book.

Note: Please consult with a lawyer or legal expert to ensure the accuracy and completeness of the copyright page for your specific circumstances.

Introduction

Welcome to "Breaking the Darkness: A Journey of Healing and Recovery from Depression." This book is a guiding light for those who are seeking solace, support, and a roadmap to navigate the often challenging path of depression and its journey towards healing.

Depression is a complex and pervasive mental health condition that affects millions of people worldwide. Its impact can be far-reaching, infiltrating every aspect of an individual's life and causing immense emotional, mental, and physical turmoil. It is a darkness that can engulf one's spirit, making it difficult to see a way out or imagine a life beyond the shadows.

However, within the pages of this book, you will discover stories of hope, practical strategies, and insights that will empower you to break free from the grip of depression. Whether you are personally battling depression or supporting someone on their journey, this book will provide valuable tools, perspectives, and resources to help you on your path to healing and recovery.

In "Breaking the Darkness," we embark on a comprehensive exploration of depression, starting with a deep understanding of its various forms, signs, and symptoms. We debunk common misconceptions and stigma surrounding depression, shedding light on the truth behind this often-misunderstood condition.

We delve into the causes and triggers of depression, examining the interplay of biological, psychological, and environmental factors. We explore the role of genetics, life events, trauma, and other stressors, helping you unravel the intricate web of influences that contribute to depression.

Recognizing the importance of seeking professional help, we guide you through the process of reaching out for support. We shed light on the role of mental health professionals, various therapy options, and overcoming common barriers that may hinder seeking help. You will gain valuable insights into therapy techniques, medications, and the essential role of self-care in the recovery journey.

As you progress through the chapters, you will explore the transformative power of self-care and lifestyle changes. We delve into nurturing your physical health, incorporating mindfulness and relaxation techniques, and fostering a healthy support system. You will discover the significance of cognitive restructuring, mindset shifts, and gratitude in transforming negative thought patterns and embracing a positive outlook.

The book goes beyond traditional therapy approaches, examining alternative and complementary therapies, nutrition, and the role of spirituality and mindfulness in promoting well-being. We tackle the barriers to recovery, address the dynamics of care giving, and offer guidance on supporting loved ones with depression.

The journey to break the darkness of depression may not be linear, and setbacks are a natural part of the process. But with the knowledge, tools, and support shared within these pages, you will find the strength and determination to persevere. Each chapter is designed to empower you, offering practical strategies, expert insights, and inspiration to guide you towards a life of renewed hope, meaning, and well-being.

Remember, you are not defined by your depression. You are a resilient individual capable of healing and embracing a brighter future. So, let us embark on this transformative journey together, Breaking the Darkness and stepping into a life filled with light, joy, and renewed purpose.

Chapter 1

Understanding Depression

Depression is a complex and pervasive mental health condition that affects millions of individuals worldwide. To embark on a journey of healing and recovery, it is crucial to have a solid understanding of depression in all its dimensions. This chapter aims to provide a comprehensive overview, from defining depression and its various forms to exploring its impact on mental, emotional, and physical well-being.

Depression can be described as a mood disorder characterized by persistent feelings of sadness, hopelessness, and a loss of interest or pleasure in activities once enjoyed. It goes beyond the ordinary ups and downs of life, lingering for weeks, months, or even years. Major Depressive Disorder (MDD) is the most common form of depression, while other forms include Persistent Depressive Disorder (PDD), Seasonal Affective Disorder (SAD), and Postpartum Depression (PPD).

Recognizing the signs and symptoms of depression is essential for early detection and intervention. While each person's experience may vary, common symptoms include persistent sadness, feelings of emptiness, loss of energy, changes in appetite and sleep patterns, difficulty concentrating, and recurring thoughts of death or suicide. It is crucial to note that depression affects individuals differently, and symptoms can manifest in a multitude of ways.

Unfortunately, depression is often misunderstood, leading to misconceptions and stigma surrounding the condition. Debunking these misconceptions is crucial for promoting understanding and empathy. One common misconception is that depression is a sign of weakness or a character flaw. In reality, depression is a medical condition rooted in complex biological, psychological, and environmental factors. It is not a choice, and individuals cannot simply "snap out of it" or "think positively" to overcome it.

The stigma surrounding depression often adds an additional layer of burden to those already struggling. Stigma perpetuates silence and shame, preventing individuals from seeking help and support. It is essential to challenge this stigma and foster a culture of acceptance and compassion, recognizing that depression is a legitimate illness deserving of understanding and support.

Depression takes a toll on various aspects of a person's well-being, affecting mental, emotional, and physical health. Mentally, depression can lead to cognitive impairments, such as difficulty concentrating, memory problems, and indecisiveness. Emotionally, individuals may experience a persistent sense of sadness, irritability, guilt, or anxiety.

Physically, depression can manifest as changes in appetite and weight, sleep disturbances, fatigue, and unexplained physical pain.

Furthermore, depression can have a profound impact on relationships, work or academic performance, and overall quality of life. It often creates a sense of isolation and disconnect, making it challenging to engage in social activities or maintain healthy relationships. The cumulative effects of depression can be overwhelming, affecting every facet of life.

By understanding depression in its entirety, individuals can develop a greater sense of empathy and self-awareness. Recognizing the signs and symptoms enables early intervention and support, facilitating the journey towards healing and recovery. Moreover, debunking misconceptions and combating stigma promotes a more inclusive and compassionate society.

Chapter 2

Unveiling the Causes and Triggers

BREAKING THE DARKNESS : A JOURNEY OF HEALING AND RECOVERY FROM DEPRESSION

Depression is a multifaceted condition influenced by a combination of biological, psychological, and environmental factors. By understanding the underlying causes and triggers, individuals can gain insight into their own experiences and develop targeted strategies for healing and recovery. This chapter aims to explore these factors, including genetics, life events, trauma, and the interplay between depression and other mental health conditions.

Biological factors play a significant role in the development of depression. Research suggests that imbalances in brain chemistry, particularly involving neurotransmitters like serotonin, norepinephrine, and dopamine, can contribute to depressive symptoms. Additionally, structural and functional abnormalities in specific brain regions, such as the prefrontal cortex and hippocampus, have been associated with depression. Hormonal imbalances, such as those occurring during periods of hormonal fluctuation or thyroid dysfunction, can also impact mood and contribute to depression.

Genetics and family history are vital considerations when exploring the causes of depression. Studies have shown that individuals with a family history of depression are more likely to experience depression themselves. Genetic factors contribute to the vulnerability to depression, although it's important to note that having a genetic predisposition does not guarantee the development of depression. Various genes have been identified as potential contributors, but the interplay between genetic factors and environmental influences is complex and still being researched.

Life events, trauma, and stressors can serve as triggers for depression. Major life changes such as loss of a loved one, divorce, job loss, or financial difficulties can significantly impact mental health and increase the risk of depression. Traumatic experiences, such as physical or emotional abuse, neglect, or witnessing violence, can also have long-lasting effects on mental well-being. Chronic stressors, such as ongoing relationship difficulties or work-related stress, can gradually contribute to the development of depression.

Depression often coexists with other mental health conditions. There is a complex relationship between depression and disorders such as anxiety, substance abuse, eating disorders, and post-traumatic stress disorder (PTSD). It is not uncommon for individuals to experience multiple conditions simultaneously, as they may share underlying risk factors or exacerbate each other's symptoms. Recognizing and addressing these comorbid conditions is essential for comprehensive treatment and recovery.

Environmental factors, including one's upbringing, social support network, and socioeconomic status, also contribute to depression. Adverse childhood experiences, such as neglect, abuse, or a lack of stable attachments, can increase the risk of developing depression later in life. A lack of supportive relationships and a sense of isolation can contribute to the onset and maintenance of depressive symptoms. Additionally, socioeconomic factors, such as poverty, unemployment, or limited access to healthcare, can significantly impact mental health outcomes.

By unveiling the causes and triggers of depression, individuals can gain a deeper understanding of their unique experiences. Recognizing the interplay between biological, psychological, and environmental factors helps to contextualize depression and reduce self-blame. This knowledge also informs treatment approaches, as it allows for tailored interventions that address the specific contributing factors.

Chapter 3

Seeking Professional Help

Seeking professional help is a vital step in the journey of healing and recovery from depression. It is important to recognize that depression is a complex condition that often requires support from trained mental health professionals. This chapter explores the significance of reaching out for help, the role of mental health professionals, different therapy options, and how to overcome common barriers to seeking professional assistance.

Reaching out for support is a courageous and essential decision for individuals experiencing depression. It can be challenging to ask for help, as depression often comes with feelings of shame, guilt, or a sense of being a burden to others. However, reaching out is a crucial step towards receiving the care and support needed to navigate the challenges of depression. It is important to remember that seeking help is not a sign of weakness but a courageous act of self-care.

Mental health professionals, such as psychiatrists, psychologists, therapists, and counsellors, play a vital role in the treatment of depression. They possess the knowledge, expertise, and skills to assess, diagnose, and provide evidence-based interventions. These professionals create a safe and non-judgmental space for individuals to explore their emotions, thoughts, and experiences. They work collaboratively with clients to develop personalized treatment plans that address the unique needs and goals of each individual.

Therapy is a cornerstone of depression treatment, and various therapeutic approaches have proven effective. Cognitive-Behavioural Therapy (CBT) focuses on identifying and challenging negative thought patterns and behaviours, replacing them with more positive and adaptive ones. Interpersonal Therapy (IPT) emphasizes the importance of relationships and helps individuals improve their communication skills, resolve conflicts, and build a supportive social network. Other therapeutic modalities, such as psychodynamic therapy, acceptance and commitment therapy (ACT), and dialectical behaviour therapy (DBT), may also be utilized based on individual needs.

In some cases, medication may be recommended as part of the treatment plan for depression. Antidepressant medications can help regulate brain chemistry and alleviate depressive symptoms. Psychiatric professionals, such as psychiatrists or primary care physicians, prescribe and monitor the use of medication. It is important to have open and honest communication with healthcare providers about the benefits, potential side effects, and any concerns or questions regarding medication.

There are common barriers that can hinder individuals from seeking professional help. These barriers include stigma, lack of awareness about available resources, financial concerns, and logistical challenges. Overcoming these barriers is crucial for accessing the support needed. Education and advocacy play a significant role in combating stigma and raising awareness about mental health.

Many communities offer low-cost or sliding-scale mental health services, and organizations provide helplines and online resources. Exploring available options, seeking financial assistance if necessary, and prioritizing mental health can help overcome logistical and financial challenges.

It is important to remember that seeking professional help is not a one-size-fits-all process. Each person's journey is unique, and finding the right mental health professional and treatment approach may require some exploration and trial. It is okay to seek second opinions and switch therapists if needed. The goal is to find a supportive and trusting therapeutic relationship that empowers and facilitates healing.

In conclusion, seeking professional help is a crucial step in the journey of healing and recovery from depression. Mental health professionals offer guidance, support, and evidence-based interventions to address the complexities of depression. Therapy options such as CBT and IPT, along with medication when appropriate, can significantly improve outcomes.

By understanding the importance of seeking help, recognizing the role of mental health professionals, and addressing barriers, individuals can take active steps towards their well-being and reclaiming their lives from the grip of depression.

Chapter 4

Self-Care and Lifestyle Changes

In the journey of healing and recovery from depression, self-care and lifestyle changes play a significant role in promoting well-being and enhancing mental health. This chapter explores the importance of nurturing physical health, incorporating mindfulness and relaxation techniques, engaging in hobbies and leisure activities, and establishing a healthy support system.

Nurturing physical health is a vital aspect of self-care when dealing with depression. Engaging in regular exercise has been shown to improve mood, increase energy levels, and reduce symptoms of depression. It can be as simple as taking a walk, practising yoga, or participating in a sport or exercise class that brings joy and a sense of accomplishment.

Prioritizing adequate sleep and establishing healthy sleep habits is also crucial, as quality sleep supports emotional regulation and overall well-being. Additionally, adopting a balanced and nutritious diet can positively impact mood and energy levels, ensuring the body receives the necessary nutrients for optimal functioning.

Exploring mindfulness, meditation, and relaxation techniques can provide valuable tools for managing depression. Mindfulness involves paying attention to the present moment with non-judgmental awareness. Practising mindfulness can help individuals cultivate a sense of calm, reduce rumination, and improve emotional regulation. Meditation, whether through guided practices or silent reflection, can promote relaxation and enhance self-awareness.

Various relaxation techniques, such as deep breathing exercises, progressive muscle relaxation, or engaging in calming activities like taking a bath or listening to soothing music, can also help reduce stress and promote a sense of tranquillity.

Engaging in hobbies, creativity, and leisure activities can have a profound impact on mood and overall well-being. Pursuing activities that bring joy, satisfaction, and a sense of accomplishment can help counteract feelings of sadness and hopelessness.

This could involve exploring artistic outlets like painting, writing, or playing a musical instrument. Engaging in hobbies can provide a much-needed distraction, promote a sense of purpose, and foster a positive sense of self-identity outside of depression.

Establishing a healthy support system and fostering meaningful connections is crucial for individuals experiencing depression. Building a network of supportive and understanding individuals who can offer emotional support, encouragement, and empathy is invaluable. This may include family members, friends, support groups, or mental health professionals.

Connecting with others who have similar experiences can provide a sense of validation, reduce feelings of isolation, and offer practical insights for managing depression. Additionally, developing healthy boundaries and seeking professional help when needed are essential aspects of maintaining a healthy support system.

It is important to note that self-care and lifestyle changes are not a substitute for professional treatment but complement it. They are tools individuals can incorporate into their daily lives to support their mental health and well-being. Experimenting with different self-care strategies and finding what works best for each individual is key. It may require some trial and error, as what works for one person may not work for another. The goal is to develop a personalized self-care routine that supports mental and emotional health.

In conclusion, self-care and lifestyle changes are integral components of the journey towards healing and recovery from depression. Nurturing physical health, practising mindfulness and relaxation techniques, engaging in hobbies, and establishing a healthy support system all contribute to overall well-being. By incorporating these self-care strategies into daily life, individuals can enhance their resilience, improve mood, and cultivate a sense of empowerment in their journey to overcome depression.

Chapter 5

Cognitive Restructuring and Mindset Shifts

Cognitive restructuring and mindset shifts are powerful tools for transforming the way we think, perceive ourselves, and approach life. In the context of depression, these techniques can help challenge negative thoughts, cultivate self-compassion, develop resilience, and harness the power of gratitude and mindfulness. This chapter explores the importance of cognitive restructuring and mindset shifts in the journey of healing and recovery.

Challenging negative thoughts and self-talk patterns is a fundamental aspect of cognitive restructuring. Depression often distorts our thinking, leading to negative interpretations and self-defeating beliefs. By becoming aware of these thoughts and actively questioning their accuracy, individuals can challenge and reframe them into more balanced and realistic perspectives. This process involves examining evidence, considering alternative explanations, and consciously choosing more positive and constructive interpretations.

Practising self-compassion is crucial in fostering a positive mindset and nurturing self-worth. Individuals experiencing depression often engage in self-criticism, blame, and harsh judgments. Cultivating self-compassion involves treating oneself with kindness, understanding, and acceptance, just as one would offer support and empathy to a loved one facing similar struggles. It entails acknowledging one's pain and imperfections while embracing a sense of inherent worth and value.

Developing resilience and coping skills is essential for managing setbacks and navigating the challenges of depression. Resilience involves the ability to adapt, bounce back, and maintain a sense of well-being in the face of adversity. It can be cultivated through various strategies, such as fostering a growth mindset, setting realistic goals, building problem-solving skills, and seeking support when needed.

Coping skills, such as effective stress management, emotional regulation, and healthy coping mechanisms, empower individuals to navigate difficult emotions and situations in a healthy and adaptive manner.

Harnessing the power of gratitude and mindfulness can have a transformative impact on daily life. Gratitude involves consciously recognizing and appreciating the positive aspects of life, no matter how small. Cultivating a gratitude practice, such as keeping a gratitude journal or regularly expressing appreciation, can shift focus away from negativity and foster a greater sense of contentment and well-being.

Mindfulness, on the other hand, involves bringing non-judgmental awareness to the present moment. By practising mindfulness, individuals can observe their thoughts and emotions without attachment or judgment, promoting a sense of calm, clarity, and self-acceptance.

Mindset shifts are not an instant fix but a gradual process that requires consistent practice and effort. It is important to approach this journey with patience, self-compassion, and an understanding that progress may come in small steps. Cognitive restructuring and mindset shifts are skills that can be honed over time, leading to a more positive and adaptive way of thinking.

In conclusion, cognitive restructuring and mindset shifts are transformative tools for individuals experiencing depression. Challenging negative thoughts, cultivating self-compassion, developing resilience, and embracing gratitude and mindfulness can significantly impact one's mindset and overall well-being.

By actively engaging in these practices, individuals can reframe their perspectives, develop healthier thinking patterns, and navigate their journey of healing and recovery with greater empowerment and resilience. Remember, change begins with a single thought, and with commitment and practice, positive mindset shifts can lead to profound transformation.

Chapter 6

Healing Through Therapy Techniques

Therapy techniques offer valuable tools and strategies to aid in the healing and recovery process from depression. This chapter explores various therapeutic modalities, including cognitive-behavioural therapy (CBT), acceptance and commitment therapy (ACT), dialectical behaviour therapy (DBT), and other therapeutic approaches that can assist individuals on their journey.

Cognitive-behavioural therapy (CBT) is a widely recognized and effective therapeutic modality for depression. CBT focuses on the relationship between thoughts, emotions, and behaviours. By identifying and challenging negative or distorted thinking patterns, individuals can gain insight into the impact of their thoughts on their emotions and behaviours. CBT techniques involve examining evidence, developing more balanced thoughts, and implementing behavioural strategies to promote positive change.

Techniques such as cognitive restructuring, behavioural activation, and problem-solving skills are commonly used in CBT to alleviate symptoms of depression and promote long-term well-being.

Acceptance and commitment therapy (ACT) is another therapeutic approach that can be beneficial for individuals experiencing depression. ACT emphasizes the cultivation of psychological flexibility and the acceptance of difficult emotions and experiences. Instead of attempting to eliminate or suppress negative thoughts and emotions, ACT encourages individuals to develop skills for accepting them and taking committed action towards living a meaningful and fulfilling life.

Techniques in ACT include mindfulness, values clarification, and committed action, all aimed at promoting psychological resilience and well-being.

Dialectical behaviour therapy (DBT) was initially developed to treat borderline personality disorder, but it has also shown effectiveness in treating depression. DBT combines elements of cognitive-behavioural therapy with mindfulness practices and skills for emotional regulation.

DBT techniques provide individuals with tools to manage intense emotions, improve distress tolerance, and enhance interpersonal effectiveness.

Skills such as mindfulness, emotion regulation, interpersonal effectiveness, and distress tolerance are central to DBT and can be highly beneficial for individuals experiencing depression.

While CBT, ACT, and DBT are well-established therapeutic modalities, there are other approaches that may also be useful in the treatment of depression. Psychodynamic therapy explores the influence of past experiences and relationships on present emotions and behaviours, helping individuals gain insight into unresolved conflicts and patterns. Interpersonal therapy (IPT) focuses on improving interpersonal relationships and resolving conflicts that may contribute to depressive symptoms.

Mindfulness-based cognitive therapy (MBCT) combines mindfulness practices with cognitive therapy techniques, specifically designed to prevent relapse in individuals with a history of depression.

Each therapeutic modality offers unique benefits, and the choice of approach depends on individual needs and preferences. It is important to work collaboratively with a trained therapist to determine the most suitable therapy technique or combination of techniques. Therapists may also integrate elements from different modalities to create a personalized treatment plan tailored to the specific needs of each individual.

In conclusion, therapy techniques provide individuals with valuable tools and strategies for healing and recovering from depression. Cognitive-behavioural therapy (CBT), acceptance and commitment therapy (ACT), dialectical behaviour therapy (DBT), and other therapeutic approaches offer effective interventions to challenge negative thoughts, enhance emotional regulation, promote acceptance, and cultivate psychological flexibility.

Each therapeutic modality has its own strengths, and the choice of approach should be based on individual circumstances and preferences. By actively engaging in therapy and incorporating these techniques into daily life, individuals can empower themselves to overcome depression and cultivate long-lasting well-being.

Chapter 7

<u>Building a Supportive Environment</u>

Building a supportive environment is crucial in the journey of healing and recovery from depression. This chapter explores the importance of navigating relationships with family and friends, communicating effectively about depression, addressing the impact of depression on intimate relationships, and building a network of support through peer groups and communities.

When dealing with depression, it is essential to navigate relationships with family and friends in a supportive and understanding manner. Educating loved ones about depression can help them grasp the nature of the condition and provide appropriate support. Open and honest communication is key, allowing individuals to express their needs, concerns, and feelings.

Family and friends can play a vital role by offering empathy, encouragement, and practical assistance. It is important to remember that not everyone may fully understand depression, so patience and understanding are crucial in fostering supportive relationships.

Communicating effectively about depression is essential in seeking the support needed. Sharing one's experiences and emotions can help loved ones better understand the challenges faced. Clearly expressing specific needs, such as the desire for company, a listening ear, or help with daily tasks, can facilitate a supportive response.

Offering educational resources or inviting loved ones to therapy sessions can also help them gain insight into depression and its impact. Effective communication ensures that individuals feel heard, validated, and supported by their loved ones.

Depression can significantly impact intimate relationships, often placing strain on the partnership. It is important to address these challenges openly and honestly. Both partners should work together to establish open lines of communication, allowing for a safe space to discuss concerns and emotions. Patience, empathy, and understanding are crucial in navigating the ups and downs of depression within the relationship.

Seeking couples therapy or relationship counselling can provide a supportive environment to address these issues and develop strategies for mutual support and growth.

Building a network of support through peer groups and communities can provide a sense of belonging and understanding. Connecting with individuals who have similar experiences can offer a unique level of support and validation. Support groups, either in-person or online, provide a platform to share experiences, learn from others, and gain practical insights for managing depression.

Additionally, online communities, forums, and social media groups can offer a sense of connection and support, especially for individuals who may have limited access to in-person resources.

Creating a supportive environment also involves setting healthy boundaries and seeking professional help when needed. Boundaries help protect one's mental and emotional well-being, ensuring that individuals have space for self-care and personal growth. Professional help, such as therapy or counselling, offers a specialized level of support and guidance to navigate the complexities of depression.

In conclusion, building a supportive environment is crucial in the journey of healing and recovery from depression. Navigating relationships with family and friends, effective communication about depression, addressing the impact on intimate relationships, and building a network of support through peer groups and communities all contribute to creating a supportive and understanding environment.

By fostering these connections and seeking appropriate support, individuals can feel empowered, understood, and less alone in their journey to overcome depression.

Chapter 8

<u>Embracing Relapse Prevention and Self-Management</u>

Embracing relapse prevention and self-management is an integral part of the journey towards long-term healing and recovery from depression. This chapter explores the importance of recognizing the risk of relapse, creating a relapse prevention plan, identifying triggers and early warning signs, developing strategies for self-management during challenging times, and emphasizing the importance of ongoing self-care and maintenance.

Recognizing the risk of relapse is a crucial step in maintaining one's mental well-being. Depression can be a chronic condition with the potential for recurrence. By understanding this risk, individuals can proactively work towards preventing relapse. It is essential to be aware of the personal factors, such as stress, life changes, or loss, that may contribute to relapse.

Creating a relapse prevention plan involves developing a set of strategies and coping mechanisms to address these triggers and minimize their impact.

Identifying triggers and early warning signs is a key aspect of relapse prevention. Triggers are events, situations, or circumstances that can provoke negative emotions or thoughts and potentially lead to a depressive episode. By identifying these triggers, individuals can be better prepared to manage them. Early warning signs are subtle changes in thoughts, feelings, or behaviours that indicate the potential onset of a depressive episode.

Recognizing these signs enables individuals to take proactive steps towards self-management and seek appropriate support when needed.

Developing strategies for self-management during challenging times empowers individuals to take control of their mental well-being. These strategies can include self-care practices, such as maintaining a healthy lifestyle with regular exercise, sufficient sleep, and a balanced diet. Engaging in activities that bring joy, practising stress reduction techniques, and seeking social support are also valuable strategies.

Additionally, cognitive and behavioural techniques, such as cognitive restructuring, relaxation exercises, and engaging in positive self-talk, can help manage negative emotions and thoughts during difficult periods.

The importance of ongoing self-care and maintenance cannot be overstated. Self-care should be viewed as an essential component of maintaining overall well-being, even when depression symptoms are in remission. Consistently practising self-care routines and prioritizing one's mental, emotional, and physical health helps build resilience and reduces the risk of relapse. It is important to regularly assess and adjust self-care strategies to meet changing needs and circumstances.

Building a support network is also crucial in relapse prevention and self-management. Trusted family members, friends, therapists, or support groups can provide invaluable support during challenging times. Regular check-ins, open communication, and reaching out for help when needed contribute to a strong support system.

Having a network of individuals who understand and validate one's experiences can significantly enhance the ability to navigate difficult periods and maintain well-being.

In conclusion, embracing relapse prevention and self-management is essential in the journey of healing and recovery from depression. Recognizing the risk of relapse, creating a relapse prevention plan, identifying triggers and early warning signs, developing strategies for self-management, and emphasizing ongoing self-care and maintenance all contribute to long-term well-being.

By actively engaging in these practices, individuals can empower themselves to navigate challenging times, minimize the risk of relapse, and cultivate a fulfilling and balanced life. Remember, self-management is an ongoing process that requires dedication and self-awareness, but with consistent effort, individuals can thrive and maintain their mental well-being.

Chapter 9

Exploring Alternative and Complementary Therapies

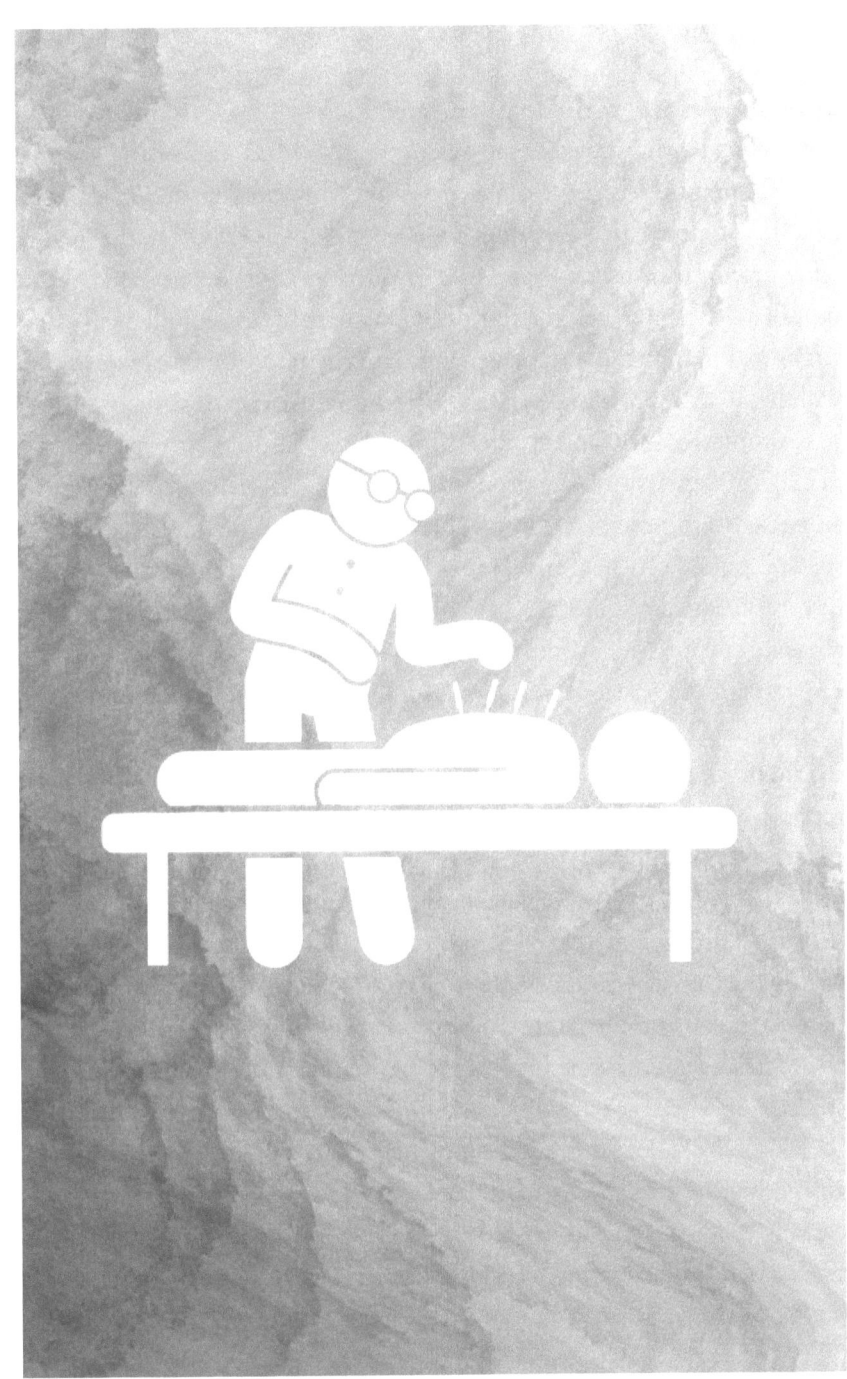

In addition to traditional therapies, there are alternative and complementary approaches that can be explored as part of the journey of healing and recovery from depression. This chapter delves into the benefits of alternative therapies such as acupuncture, yoga, and herbal remedies. It also discusses the role of nutrition and dietary changes in supporting mental health, the potential benefits of supplements and vitamins for depression management, and the importance of consulting with healthcare professionals before trying alternative treatments.

Alternative therapies offer individuals additional options for managing depression and promoting overall well-being. Acupuncture, an ancient Chinese practice, involves the insertion of thin needles into specific points on the body. It is believed to stimulate energy flow and restore balance. Some studies suggest that acupuncture may help alleviate depressive symptoms and improve overall mental health. However, more research is needed to fully understand its effectiveness in treating depression.

Yoga, a mind-body practice, combines physical postures, breath control, and meditation. Regular yoga practice has been associated with reduced symptoms of depression and anxiety. The combination of physical movement, mindfulness, and relaxation techniques in yoga can help individuals manage stress, improve mood, and cultivate a sense of well-being. Incorporating yoga into a comprehensive treatment plan can be a beneficial complement to other therapeutic approaches.

Herbal remedies, such as St. John's Wort and Saffron, have been studied for their potential benefits in managing depressive symptoms. St. John's Wort, a plant-based supplement, has shown some promise in alleviating mild to moderate depression. However, it can interact with certain medications, so consulting with a healthcare professional is crucial before considering its use. Saffron, a spice derived from the crocus flower, has also shown potential antidepressant effects.

It is important to note that herbal remedies should be used with caution and under the guidance of a healthcare professional due to potential side effects and interactions with other medications.

Nutrition and dietary changes play a significant role in supporting mental health. Research suggests that certain nutrients, such as omega-3 fatty acids, B vitamins, and minerals like zinc and magnesium, may have a positive impact on mood and overall well-being. Incorporating a balanced diet that includes foods rich in these nutrients, such as fatty fish, leafy greens, whole grains, and nuts, can be beneficial for managing depression.

However, it is important to note that diet alone is not a substitute for professional treatment, and individuals should consult with a healthcare professional or registered dietitian before making significant dietary changes.

Supplements and vitamins are commonly marketed as natural remedies for depression. Some studies have shown potential benefits of certain supplements, such as omega-3 fatty acids, SAM-e, and vitamin D, in reducing depressive symptoms. However, it is essential to consult with a healthcare professional before starting any supplements, as they can interact with medications and may not be appropriate for everyone.

Additionally, the quality and dosage of supplements vary, so it is important to choose reputable brands and follow professional recommendations.

It is crucial to emphasize the importance of consulting with healthcare professionals before trying alternative treatments. While alternative therapies can be beneficial for some individuals, they may not be suitable or effective for everyone. Healthcare professionals can provide guidance, evaluate individual circumstances, and ensure that treatments are safe and integrated into a comprehensive care plan.

They can also help individuals navigate potential interactions with medications and monitor progress.

In conclusion, exploring alternative and complementary therapies can offer additional avenues for managing depression and supporting mental health. Practices such as acupuncture and yoga, as well as herbal remedies, nutrition, and supplements, may have potential benefits in alleviating depressive symptoms.

However, it is essential to consult with healthcare professionals before trying alternative treatments, as they can provide expert guidance and ensure safe and effective integration into a comprehensive care plan.

Chapter 10

Overcoming Barriers to Recovery

In the journey of healing from depression, individuals often encounter various barriers that can impede their progress. This chapter focuses on addressing common obstacles such as feelings of guilt, shame, and self-blame, challenges related to medication management and side effects, and societal and cultural barriers to seeking help and support.

Feelings of guilt, shame, and self-blame are common emotions experienced by individuals with depression. It is important to recognize that depression is not a personal failing or a result of weakness. It is a complex condition influenced by various factors, including genetics, biology, and life experiences. Overcoming these negative emotions involves re-framing the narrative and understanding that depression is a legitimate illness that requires treatment and support.

Seeking therapy, engaging in self-compassion practices, and educating oneself about depression can help individuals challenge and overcome feelings of guilt, shame, and self-blame.

Medication management can present its own set of challenges in the recovery process. Some individuals may face concerns about starting or continuing medication due to fears of dependency, side effects, or stigma. It is essential to work closely with a healthcare professional to understand the benefits and potential risks of medication. Open communication about concerns and experiences with medications can help in finding the most effective treatment plan.

Regular check-ins and discussions with healthcare professionals can address any side effects and ensure the medication is working optimally. Additionally, exploring complementary therapies or alternative treatments alongside medication may provide a well-rounded approach to recovery.

Societal and cultural barriers can significantly impact an individual's willingness to seek help and support for depression. Stigma, lack of understanding, and cultural beliefs around mental health can create significant hurdles. Overcoming these barriers requires education and awareness campaigns to combat stigma, promote empathy, and encourage open conversations about mental health.

Community outreach programs and support networks specific to different cultures and communities can play a vital role in breaking down these barriers. By creating safe and inclusive spaces, individuals can find the support they need without fear of judgment or discrimination.

In some cultures, seeking professional help for mental health issues may be viewed as a sign of weakness or taboo. It is essential to normalize the conversation around mental health and highlight the importance of seeking help. Sharing personal stories of recovery and success can inspire others to take the necessary steps towards healing. Collaborating with community leaders, religious institutions, and local organizations can help in creating culturally sensitive and accessible mental health resources.

Increasing awareness of available support systems and highlighting success stories from diverse backgrounds can encourage individuals to seek help and overcome cultural barriers.

Addressing barriers to recovery involves a multifaceted approach that includes self-reflection, education, communication, and societal change. By challenging feelings of guilt, shame, and self-blame, individuals can break free from negative self-perceptions and embrace the healing process. Engaging in open conversations about medication management and exploring alternative treatments can provide a more personalized and effective approach to recovery.

Breaking down societal and cultural barriers through education, awareness, and support can create a more accepting and inclusive environment where individuals feel empowered to seek help and support.

In conclusion, overcoming barriers to recovery is a crucial step in the journey of healing from depression. By addressing feelings of guilt, shame, and self-blame, navigating challenges related to medication management, and overcoming societal and cultural barriers to seeking help, individuals can break free from the limitations that impede their progress.

By promoting understanding, empathy, and access to resources, we can create a supportive environment where individuals feel empowered to seek help, receive the necessary support, and embark on a path of healing and recovery from depression.

Chapter 11

Expressive Therapies for Healing

Expressive therapies offer unique and powerful ways to facilitate healing and recovery from depression. This chapter explores the therapeutic benefits of art therapy, music therapy, dance/movement therapy, journaling and writing exercises, as well as the power of storytelling and narrative therapy in the recovery process.

Art therapy provides individuals with a creative outlet for exploring and expressing their emotions. Through various art mediums, such as drawing, painting, or sculpting, individuals can externalize their inner experiences and gain insight into their emotions and thoughts. Art therapy allows for non-verbal expression, making it especially beneficial for individuals who find it challenging to articulate their feelings. Engaging in art-making can provide a sense of control, self-discovery, and empowerment, promoting healing and emotional well-being.

Music therapy utilizes the therapeutic elements of music to support healing and recovery. Listening to or creating music can evoke powerful emotions, stimulate memories, and enhance mood. Music therapy interventions may include playing instruments, singing, or composing songs. The rhythmic and melodic elements of music can help regulate emotions, reduce stress, and promote relaxation. Music therapy can also provide a sense of connection, as individuals often relate to lyrics and melodies that resonate with their own experiences.

Dance/movement therapy combines movement, body awareness, and creative expression to promote emotional and physical well-being. Through guided movement exercises and dance, individuals can explore and release emotions held in the body. Dance/movement therapy encourages self-expression, improves self-esteem, and enhances body-mind integration. It can also serve as a means of communication and connection with others, fostering a sense of belonging and support.

Journaling and writing exercises offer a therapeutic outlet for self-reflection and exploration. Writing can be a powerful tool for processing emotions, organizing thoughts, and gaining clarity. Engaging in journaling exercises allows individuals to express their feelings, document their experiences, and track their progress. Writing can also provide a sense of catharsis and serve as a personal narrative of growth and resilience.

Storytelling and narrative therapy harness the power of storytelling as a means of healing and transformation. Sharing personal stories and experiences allows individuals to create meaning, gain perspective, and reframe their narratives. Narrative therapy encourages individuals to view themselves as the authors of their stories, empowering them to rewrite and reshape their narratives in a way that promotes healing and recovery.

Storytelling can also foster a sense of connection and empathy, as it allows individuals to relate to and learn from the experiences of others.

Incorporating expressive therapies into the recovery process offers individuals alternative and creative ways to explore and address their emotional well-being. These therapies tap into the inherent human capacity for creative expression, enabling individuals to access and process emotions that may be difficult to express through traditional verbal means.

By engaging in art, music, dance, journaling, and storytelling, individuals can find unique avenues for self-discovery, emotional release, and personal growth.

It is important to note that expressive therapies can be facilitated by trained professionals, such as art therapists, music therapists, dance/movement therapists, or licensed counsellors. These professionals provide guidance, create a safe and supportive environment, and tailor interventions to meet individual needs. By working with qualified practitioners, individuals can fully benefit from the therapeutic potential of expressive therapies in their healing journey.

In conclusion, expressive therapies offer valuable tools for healing and recovery from depression. Art therapy, music therapy, dance/movement therapy, journaling and writing exercises, as well as storytelling and narrative therapy, provide individuals with creative outlets to process emotions, promote self-expression, and foster personal growth.

By incorporating these expressive modalities into the recovery process, individuals can explore and discover new dimensions of their emotional well-being, empowering them to embark on a path of healing, resilience, and renewed hope.

Chapter 12

The Role of Spirituality and Mindfulness

BREAKING THE DARKNESS : A JOURNEY OF HEALING AND RECOVERY FROM DEPRESSION

Spirituality and mindfulness play significant roles in promoting mental health and well-being. This chapter explores the connection between spirituality and mental health, delves into the role of faith, prayer, and meditation in finding solace and meaning, discusses the benefits of cultivating mindfulness practices, and highlights the importance of integrating spiritual and mindfulness practices into daily life for enhanced well-being.

Spirituality refers to a deeply personal and subjective experience that encompasses a sense of connection to something greater than oneself. It involves seeking meaning, purpose, and a sense of transcendence in life. Research has shown that spirituality can have a positive impact on mental health, providing individuals with a source of comfort, hope, and resilience.

Engaging in spiritual practices can foster a sense of belonging, provide a framework for understanding life's challenges, and offer solace during difficult times.

Faith, prayer, and meditation are integral components of many spiritual traditions and can provide individuals with a sense of inner peace and tranquillity. Faith serves as a guiding force, offering support and comfort in times of distress. Prayer allows for communication with a higher power, providing individuals with a sense of connection, gratitude, and surrender.

Meditation, on the other hand, involves cultivating a focused and non-judgmental awareness of the present moment, allowing individuals to observe their thoughts, emotions, and sensations with acceptance and equanimity.

Mindfulness practices, rooted in ancient traditions such as Buddhism, have gained recognition for their benefits in promoting mental well-being. Mindfulness involves intentionally paying attention to the present moment without judgment. By cultivating mindfulness, individuals develop self-awareness, allowing them to observe their thoughts and emotions without getting entangled in them.

This increased self-awareness can help reduce rumination, break free from automatic patterns of thinking, and enhance overall psychological flexibility.

Integrating spiritual and mindfulness practices into daily life can have profound effects on mental health and well-being. It involves incorporating moments of reflection, prayer, or meditation into one's routine, carving out dedicated time for self-care and self-reflection.

This integration can be achieved through setting aside specific periods for spiritual practices, participating in religious or spiritual gatherings, or finding ways to infuse mindfulness into everyday activities such as eating, walking, or engaging in conversations.

Incorporating spirituality and mindfulness into daily life can provide individuals with a sense of purpose, connection, and inner peace. It can offer a deeper understanding of oneself and others, foster a greater sense of compassion and gratitude, and promote overall emotional well-being.

Engaging in spiritual and mindfulness practices can serve as a source of strength, resilience, and support in navigating the challenges of life.

It is important to note that spirituality and mindfulness are highly personal and can be practised in a variety of ways. Different individuals may resonate with different spiritual traditions or mindfulness techniques. It is crucial to find approaches that align with one's beliefs, values, and preferences.

Seeking guidance from spiritual leaders, participating in mindfulness programs or retreats, and exploring various resources can help individuals find the practices that resonate most with them.

In conclusion, spirituality and mindfulness play significant roles in promoting mental health and well-being. By examining the connection between spirituality and mental health, exploring the role of faith, prayer, and meditation, cultivating mindfulness practices, and integrating spiritual and mindfulness practices into daily life, individuals can tap into a deep well of solace, meaning, and self-awareness.

Embracing spirituality and mindfulness can provide a profound sense of purpose, connection, and inner peace, enhancing overall emotional well-being and supporting the journey of healing and recovery from depression.

Chapter 13
Supporting Loved Ones with Depression

Supporting a loved one who is experiencing depression can be challenging and overwhelming. This chapter provides guidance for family and friends on how to support someone with depression, understanding the dynamics of care-giving, managing compassion fatigue, communicating effectively, and recognizing the importance of boundaries and self-care for caregivers and support systems.

When supporting a loved one with depression, it is crucial to approach them with empathy, understanding, and patience. Depression can make individuals feel isolated, misunderstood, and overwhelmed, and your support can make a significant difference in their journey of healing. Start by educating yourself about depression, its symptoms, and treatment options. This knowledge will help you gain a better understanding of what your loved one is going through.

One of the most essential aspects of supporting someone with depression is effective communication. Be an active listener, creating a safe space for your loved one to share their feelings and experiences. Avoid judgment or offering quick solutions. Instead, provide empathy and validation by acknowledging their emotions and expressing your willingness to support them. Sometimes, simply being present and offering a compassionate ear can be immensely comforting.

Care giving for someone with depression can take a toll on your own well-being. It is important to recognize the dynamics of care giving and manage compassion fatigue. Caregivers often experience emotional exhaustion, stress, and burnout. Set realistic expectations for yourself and seek support from other family members, friends, or support groups.

Taking breaks, practising self-care, and seeking your own emotional support are essential for maintaining your own well-being while supporting your loved one.

Establishing boundaries is crucial when supporting someone with depression. It is essential to recognize that you cannot single-handedly "fix" their depression. Respect their autonomy and avoid taking responsibility for their emotional well-being. Encourage them to seek professional help and offer assistance in finding suitable treatment options.

Setting boundaries also means understanding when to prioritize your own well-being. It is okay to take care of yourself and seek support if you are feeling overwhelmed.

Encourage your loved one to engage in self-care activities and maintain a healthy lifestyle. Offer assistance in finding resources, such as therapy or support groups, that can provide additional help. Encourage them to seek professional guidance, as therapists and mental health professionals can offer specialized support and treatment options. Be patient and supportive as they navigate their journey of healing and recovery.

Remember that supporting someone with depression requires ongoing effort and understanding. Be prepared for setbacks and relapses and continue to offer your support and encouragement. Encourage them to celebrate small victories and milestones along the way. Remind them that healing takes time and that you are there for them, no matter what.

In conclusion, supporting a loved one with depression requires empathy, effective communication, and an understanding of the dynamics of care giving. By offering empathy, patience, and validation, you can create a safe and supportive environment for your loved one.

Remember to prioritize your own well-being, establish boundaries, and seek support when needed. Together, you can provide the necessary support for your loved one's journey of healing and recovery from depression.

Chapter 14
Thriving Beyond Recovery

Recovery from depression is not just about returning to a state of equilibrium; it is also about embracing the potential for growth, resilience, and a life of meaning and fulfilment. In this chapter, we explore the concept of post-depression growth, discuss how to embrace a life of purpose and fulfilment, set and pursue new goals and aspirations, and cultivate self-compassion while celebrating progress in the journey of thriving beyond recovery.

Post-depression growth refers to the positive transformation that can occur as a result of overcoming depression. It involves building resilience, developing a new perspective on life, and discovering inner strengths and resources that were previously untapped. Recognizing that the journey of recovery can lead to personal growth and positive change is a powerful mindset shift that can empower individuals to move forward with hope and optimism.

Embracing a life of meaning, purpose, and fulfilment is an integral part of thriving beyond recovery. It involves reflecting on one's values, passions, and interests and aligning them with the choices and actions taken in daily life. Engaging in activities that bring joy, fulfilment, and a sense of purpose can provide a sense of direction and satisfaction.

This could involve pursuing hobbies, volunteering, or engaging in meaningful work that contributes to the well-being of oneself and others.

Setting new goals and aspirations is an important step in the journey of thriving beyond recovery. These goals can be both big and small, serving as stepping stones towards a more fulfilling life. Start by identifying areas of interest or areas where personal growth is desired.

Break these larger goals into smaller, manageable steps and celebrate each milestone along the way. Remember that progress, no matter how small, is still progress.

Cultivating self-compassion is vital in the process of thriving beyond recovery. Treat yourself with kindness, understanding, and acceptance. Acknowledge the challenges faced during the journey of recovery and celebrate the resilience and progress made. Practice self-care and self-compassion by prioritizing activities that nurture your physical, mental, and emotional well-being.

Allow yourself to rest, recharge, and engage in activities that bring you joy and fulfilment.

As you progress on your journey of thriving beyond recovery, remember that setbacks may occur. It is essential to maintain a mindset of resilience and flexibility. When faced with challenges, reflect on the progress you have made so far and draw upon the strategies and resources that have been effective in the past. Surround yourself with a supportive network of friends, family, or support groups who can provide encouragement and understanding.

Celebrate your progress along the way. Recognize and appreciate the growth and positive changes that have occurred in your life. Take time to reflect on the resilience and strength you have developed throughout the recovery process. Cultivate gratitude for the lessons learned, the support received, and the opportunities for personal growth that have emerged.

In conclusion, thriving beyond recovery involves embracing the concept of post-depression growth, pursuing a life of meaning and fulfilment, setting new goals and aspirations, and cultivating self-compassion while celebrating progress. Remember that the journey of thriving is unique for each individual.

Embrace the opportunities for personal growth, discover new passions and purpose, and continue to nurture your well-being as you move forward on your path of thriving beyond recovery.

Conclusion

As we come to the end of "Breaking the Darkness: A Journey of Healing and Recovery from Depression," we hope that this book has provided you with the guidance, support, and inspiration needed to navigate the challenging path of depression. Throughout these pages, we have explored the depths of depression and uncovered the possibilities of healing and transformation.

Depression is a formidable adversary, but you are stronger than you realize. The journey of healing and recovery may be filled with ups and downs, but remember that setbacks do not define your ultimate destination. Every step, no matter how small, brings you closer to a life of renewed hope, purpose, and well-being.

We have explored the importance of seeking professional help, engaging in therapy, and breaking down the barriers that hinder seeking support. We have delved into the power of self-care and lifestyle changes, highlighting the significance of physical health, mindfulness, and building a supportive network. We have examined the role of cognitive restructuring, alternative therapies, and the importance of spirituality and mindfulness in fostering healing.

In closing, we want to emphasize that healing from depression is not a linear process. There may be setbacks, moments of doubt, and days when the darkness feels overwhelming. But remember that you possess an inherent strength and resilience within you. By implementing the strategies and insights shared in this book, you have equipped yourself with the tools to navigate these challenges and emerge stronger.

As you continue on your journey, be patient with yourself. Celebrate each small victory and remember that progress is not always measured in leaps and bounds but in the small steps taken every day towards a brighter future. Surround yourself with a supportive community, lean on your loved ones, and reach out for professional help when needed.

Never forget that your story matters. Your experiences, struggles, and triumphs can inspire others who may be walking a similar path. By sharing your journey, you can become a beacon of hope for those still navigating the darkness.

Remember, you are not defined by your depression. You are a resilient individual, capable of breaking free from the darkness and embracing a life of healing, growth, and fulfilment. With perseverance, self-compassion, and the support of others, you have the power to create a future that surpasses your wildest dreams.

Please do not forget to leave a review for this book. Because reviews help me to help more people.

As you embark on the road ahead, may you find strength in knowing that you are not alone. Together, let us continue to break the darkness and forge a path towards a brighter tomorrow.

Dr. Jilesh
  www.psychologyquill.com[1]
  www.healingoraclewisdom.com[2]

---

1. http://www.psychologyquill.com/
2. http://www.healingoraclewisdom.com/

www.ingramcontent.com/pod-product-compliance
Ingram Content Group UK Ltd.
Pitfield, Milton Keynes, MK11 3LW, UK
UKHW041948230426
12048UKWH00008B/208